I LIFT MY EYES

Inspirational Short Stories to Soothe the Soul

Ann Miner

Cover and author photos by Kat Miner

Copyright © 2012 Ann Miner
All rights reserved.

ISBN: 0615664237
ISBN 13: 9780615664231

*This book is dedicated to the
Memory of
Burton Wayne Wadsworth 1924 -2008*

ACKNOWLEDGEMENTS

I gratefully acknowledge all who have encouraged me, over the years, to write a book, and those who have prayed specifically for me to get it done. You are many, and you know who you are. Thank you for believing in me.

I am grateful to my daughter, Kat Miner. Her encouragement kept me going when I was doubtful or in a slump. Her invaluable technical help kept my hysterics to a minimum.

I am indebted to Marilyn King and David Spillman, both accomplished authors, who commented specifically about a certain segment of my book that was better than all the rest, and explained why. They paved my path to better writing.

Thanks, also, to Wendy Ball, Kat Miner and others who saved some of the pieces I had e-mailed, and copied them to me when my computer was stolen. They got me out of the closet, where I was curled up in the fetal position, sucking my thumb for the loss of my writing.

Thanks, also, to members of the California Writers' Club, High Desert branch. The advice and inspiration of our published authors have kept me convicted.

Lastly, my gratitude to Burt Wadsworth, my precious husband, who loved me, inspired me, and guided me into an awesome arena of prayer and spirituality that changed my life and my relationship with God forever.

TABLE OF CONTENTS

Prologue ix
Daddy and Me 1
Ole Hank 3
The Gift of Newness 7
Returning From Exile 9
Impact 11
Basket of Wisdom 13
Bloom Where You Are Planted 15
Adopted 19
Be Content Wherever You Are 23
Fire! 25
Broken Chains 27
Spaghetti Sauce and Joy 29
Solid Gold 31
Dad 33
Sandra 35
Get In the Boat 37
God Knew 39
Not Yet 41
Grace and Mercy 43
Sister-Friends 45
Suzanne 51
Ask 53
Reminiscing 55
Intercessory Prayer 57
"I Promise" 59
What Could Go Wrong in Spring?! 65
Mercies 67
Winter Is Coming! 69

I LIFT MY EYES
By Ann Miner

PROLOGUE

For we are God's workmanship, created in Christ Jesus to do good works, which God prepared in advance for us to do. Ephesians 2:10

...He who began a good work in you will carry it on to completion... Philippians 1:6

People have told me for years that I should write a book. My inspiration comes from life. I believe that we all have a book in us. While our lives are unique to our own experiences, we can find similarity with one another. We all have drama and trauma, and each of us has a story to tell.

I sincerely believe that the stories here are what God has called me to share for now. I prayed about what to include, and realize that there will be another book to follow, as He leads me to other arenas.

Meanwhile, it is my prayer that at least one story within will touch a heart in a significant and positive way, as the reader finds familiarity in the pilgrimage toward heaven.

I lift my eyes to the hills – where does my help come from? My help comes from the Lord, the Maker of heaven and earth. Psalm 121:1

DADDY AND ME

It was a cool, crisp fall morning, before dawn. I slithered out of my cozy sleeping bag, plucked my clothes from the wooden rocker and scurried over the cold, bare floor into the living room of the old cabin. The warmth of the roaring fire in the large rock fireplace caressed my skin as I pulled jeans up over long johns, and tugged hiking boots on over thick, wool socks. The aroma of sizzling bacon and sweet pancakes cooking on the wood-burning stove in the kitchen promised a favorite breakfast. But it would have to wait. Daddy and I were going to the duck blind!

I was a blonde, curly-headed seven-year-old girl, and I was very excited on this special morning. We bundled up in snug woolen jackets and descended the stone steps of the Upper Cabin of Kiowa Lake. We hiked down the grassy hillside, in the gray-blue pre-dawn mist. Daddy carried a Thermos of hot chocolate, and held onto my mitten-covered hand.

At the bottom of the hill, we came to a remote inlet of the large lake, where we spotted the duck blind, surrounded by tall, elegant Cattails, their fuzzy brown heads gently moving in the awakening morning air. The blind was a small, wooden structure, built on stilts, and sitting low over the brownish muddy water.

The old gray paint was blistered and peeling after years of exposure to the harsh Oklahoma weather. We tiptoed across the narrow, slatted landing, opened the small flap of a door and entered our tiny hideaway. Inside, we could hear the water lapping lazily against the wooden floor. The faint stench of decaying crayfish carcasses was quickly overcome by the familiar mingling smells of other water life - that fishy odor that even if you could not hear the sloshing water or see the lively minnows darting through the reeds - you would realize that you were at water's edge.

There was just enough room for the two of us - with Daddy crouching down and me standing on tiptoe - to peer out the tiny slits that afforded our clandestine view of the lake. From this vantage point, we could see any ducks that might come near. Daddy poured steaming hot chocolate into our shared thermos cup, and we traded sips of the creamy drink while we waited silently for our first sighting.

For the Lord your God will bless you...and your joy will be complete. Deuteronomy 15:16

OLE HANK

He was a good man, smart and honest. His full name was Henry Lee Rowley. In the little Southeast Oklahoma town of Kiowa, where he grew up, townsfolk pronounced his name "Henner Lee." I called him Uncle.

In addition to being an avid and talented tennis player, he was a wonderful, self-taught piano player. When he stretched out his hands to play, the air filled with harmonic, full tones, in a sort of rinkytink style.

I liked to stand beside him when I was little, at the left end of the piano, to watch and listen. Since I knew how to play the piano, too, he called out the corresponding low notes for me to plunk along with him. I loved this exercise.

He worked in the grocery store that my dad – his brother - owned. He did a bit of everything but the butcher shop, like the rest of the employees. Another Henry was in charge of the meats.

How well I remember his high energy, his sense of humor, the sparkle in his eyes, and the practical jokes he liked to play on this little niece!

He fooled me more than once when he called to me as I was leaving the store through the back door. "Come here," he called. When I got to him he would ask, "How far would you have been if I hadn't called you back?"

Our little town of Kiowa was peaceful. Of course, everyone knew everyone else. There were farmers and ranchers, merchants and housewives, teachers and laborers. There was a cotton gin on one side of town, anda sawmill on the other. One school housed all twelve grades. The "picture show" was the main form of entertainment, unless there was a barn dance on Saturday night.

Streets throughout the township were gravel. Homes were on large properties, some with picket fences. Henry Lee and his wife and two young children lived near the school, and across the road from his mother, my grandmother.

The youngest of nine siblings, Henry Lee was eventually the last Rowley remaining in Kiowa. He decided to move his young family to Liberal, Kansas, to live near his sister and her husband.

After he retired, he referred to himself as Ole Hank, and that is how folks there remember him.

He was a great tennis player. Many of the locals, youth and adults alike, came to the courts for free instructions from Hank. He showed up at the courts daily until he was 85 or so, then continued three days a week for a few more years. His "business" card read, "Ole Hank - oldest tennis player in Liberal since 1983." I never asked who died in 1983 to make him the oldest.

He was an amateur photographer, and a camera was his constant-companion. He walked all through town, going into places of business, getting people to smile for his camera. After he developed the photos in duplicate, he tracked the folks down to share a copy of them. On the back of each photo, in big black pen, he printed names of the subjects, the date and address of the location where he snapped the picture, and a little something personal. For instance, "John Wilson and Larry Jones, having coffee and cake at Wheelers' Cafe, 311 Elm, Liberal, Kansas, on January 9, 1989. Real nice folks."

The one photo I remember vividly is the one he mailed to me. It was of his sister, my Aunt Estelle, lying in her casket at the funeral home. It was not something I would have requested, but I found it so interesting and so like Uncle Henry Lee. On the back of the picture he stated her name, date of birth, date of death, the name and address of the funeral home, the name and license number of the embalmer -and what a good job he did - and who of the family attended the funeral. I do not have to wonder how Aunt Estelle might have felt about being photographed lying in state.

Eventually, Ole Hank had so many boxes filled with photos that he ran out of space to store them in his little house. He built a storage shed solely for storing the boxes filled with the hundreds - or perhaps thousands - of images of the locals.

The local television station did a special on Ole Hank. It showed him playing tennis, playing the piano, taking pictures. The program included interviews with the mayor, the chief of police, the publisher of the newspaper, and others who knew and respected him.

In 2000, they named the new tennis complex "The Henry Lee Rowley Tennis Courts" - and people came from all over the country to commemorate the occasion. Some were leaders in the U.S. government; some owned corporations; others were at the top in their industries. His grandsons spoke, one tennis pro, the other a pastor. All of them had been taught tennis by Ole Hank. Each of them talked about how his teaching and leading was much more about life than about tennis. They said their successes in life traced back to the moral foundations laid by Hank while they played tennis.

At the end of the ceremony, they invited Ole Hank to speak. People waited in anticipation of what this good man would say. He came to the microphone and spoke only a few sentences, humbly thanking everyone. He finished with something I will never forget.

"But the important thing," he said, "is get to know Jesus as quick as you can." Then he sat back down.

Get to know Jesus as quick as you can. That's all we need to do. The rest will take care of itself.

After his sister died, and later his wife, Ole Hank hung up his tennis racket, packed up his camera, and moved to a rest home. The residents there loved hearing him play favorite old hymns on his piano - which he took with him.

He lived 97 years. Years of glorifying God, of telling people about Jesus. As we cousins and kin gathered around at his burial, none could ever recall seeing Henry Lee angry. We only remembered the laughing eyes, the sweet smile, and the gentle spirit…and we rejoiced. For this loved and loving soul was finally home with his Jesus. Amen

"My son, do not forget my teaching, but keep my commands in your heart, for they will prolong your life many years, and bring you prosperity.

Let love and faithfulness never leave you; bind them around your neck, write them on the tablet of your heart. Then you will win favor and a good name in the sight of God and man.

Trust in the Lord with all your heart and lean not on your own understanding; in all your ways acknowledge him, and he will make your paths straight." Proverbs 3:1-6

THE GIFT OF NEWNESS

I will give thanks to the Lord with all my heart;

I will tell of all Thy wonders. I will sing praise to Thy name, O Most High!

Psalm 9:1-3

It is early morning and the pale sun stretches across the tips of the greasewood, as my front yard awakens to another day. Two cottontails, frolicking like kittens, play hide and seek in the shiny green brush. The morning train snakes through the valley, wailing its greeting – two longs, a short, a long…waaaahwaaahwahwaaah!

Indian summer is over. I know that's so when I see white-crowned sparrows and juncos mingling with the other greedy birds at the feeders. They are the first to signal the cooler season, and their return brings me joy.

The change of seasons offers freshness…another opportunity to put away things of the past and move forward to new ones. Another chance for really delving into that new bible study, for planting those new bulbs, for enjoying the stillness of home as the children return to school. Another chance for goodness.*Another chance!*

Who else but the Lord could design such a pattern of seasons in our lives, with all the good and not so good that come with them. We have an opportunity to learn from every one.

What season of my year- of my life - am I in? What am I to learn from it? How am I to react?

How blessed is the one…whose delight is in the law of the Lord, and in His law he meditates day and night. And he will be like a tree firmly planted by streams of water which yields its fruit in its season, and its leaf does not wither; and in whatever he does, he prospers.

Psalm 1:2 - 3.

RETURNING FROM EXILE

"The thing I like best about myself is my humility."

We had divided into small groups to discuss what we liked best about ourselves. It seems a strange subject to me now, but I was just trying to be funny, and I did get a surprised chuckle.

Seriously, though, I prayed for humility for years. I always felt that I was too cocky, and thought that I would be kinder if I were more humble.

Years later, I returned to college out of state. God had paved a smooth path for me to get back into school after a twenty-year absence. My plans were to graduate and take that big job I had been told would be there waiting to snatch me up.

I did graduate, but instead of that big job, the economy dipped and there were no big jobs. In addition, I learned that companies preferred to hire younger people. Two different prospective employers actually told me that I was too old! I worked several part time jobs, on call, and still had problems meeting my expenses.

All the jobs had younger supervisors who did not think that a middle-aged woman had any sense. They treated me as if I were stupid. I tried unsuccessfully to fit in, but I never caught on to their way of thinking, and I felt emotionally beaten up.

"Lord, what would you have me do?" I questioned. Did humility mean that I wanted to be so broke?

I saw then that I did not want anything for myself that the Lord did not want for me. If He wanted me to live in my car, I would live in my car. I believe that was what He was waiting for. I accepted that He wanted me to experience what I had asked for, and therefore lean on Him, not on myself.

Now, oddly, I felt at peace. I told a friend that I had never been so broke and so at peace in my life. It felt good. Suddenly, I realized that I could go back home, something I had not originally intended to do. Jobs had come to me easily there. I picked up the phone and called two managers I had worked for previously, and both said they had a job for me.

With excitement, I put my house on the market and packed my car with a few things I would need until the house sold.

I had formed the habit of beginning each day with reading the "Upper Room" devotional, studying the suggested scriptures, and praying my prayer list. On the day I was leaving, I knew that I was too excited to concentrate on the scriptures. I left the Bible and little book on the kitchen counter. When the car was packed and ready to go, I went back to read and pray. I discovered that the title for that day's study was "Returning From Exile."

How appropriate. I had spent seven years in this strange city. Some were good. Some were not. Nevertheless, all of them were learning experiences that I carry with me to this day. The most important lesson of all was to trust in God.

Trust in the Lord with all your heart and lean not on your own understanding; in all ways acknowledge him and he will make your paths straight.

Proverbs 3:5, 6

IMPACT

Word of my cousin's death has reached my ears. The landscapes of our last visit are with me constantly. The aura has floated all the way here, to my home, to my realm. It will not go away.

The image of her smiling face leaps forward. She throws me a kiss as we wave goodbye. Two decades have passed since we last met. Our time has been rushed, treasured. We could not know there would be no other.

Memories come flooding back, silent waves upon silent sand. We are babes on the blanket, crawling and giggling. We are in the rowboat, wearing our little life jackets to protect us against danger. Her short, brown curls tighten in the moist air.

Older now, we splash and swim on the lake, race to the tower, never sure what the purpose of the tower is, or why it is there.

We clamor up the wooden steps that rise over the fence, our gateway to the spillway, and more adventure. Here, water moccasins and turtles, rattlesnakes and an abundance of bugs delight us, as we fearlessly drop our hooks in the water. Our cane poles are long and sturdy, strong enough to hold a black, snapping terrapin, or a snake, before the creature lets go and drops back into the safety of the dark water.

These memories and others wander through my heart as I go about my daily business.

If we knew the impact we have on others, if we knew how thoughts of us would permeate every moment of their days soon after we are gone, I wonder how we would change.

It will happen in the twinkling of an eye…those who have died will be raised to live forever. And we who are living will also be transformed.
1 Corinthians 15:52

BASKET OF WISDOM

My oldest son was about to leave home to join the Navy at the age of 18. Missing him already, I took him out to dinner for a one-on-one visit. During the meal, it occurred to me that I may not have prepared him enough for this giant leap from our secure home into the vast, overwhelming world. In fact, I was certain of that.

I told him that I wished I could fill a large basket to take with him. It would contain wisdom about how to handle all the new experiences he would encounter. I wanted it to cover anything and everything I had neglected to teach him, so that he would be protected from harm.

Since this was, of course, impossible, I had to just trust his judgment, and allow him to make his own mistakes, as I had done (and still do).

I imagine that God has a basket of wisdom for each of us, and that He allows us to take only one thing at a time off the top layer. He knows just how much we can handle at once, and He knows what we need. His provision comes just in time, (although we sometimes believe that he miscalculates)!

He loves us in the same way we love our own children. However, I suspect, Our Father's love is a great deal stronger than even we parents can ever comprehend. When we release our children to the Lord, we can achieve peace. We just have to let go, for He is so much better at parenting than we are.

For He will command His angels concerning you to guard you in all your ways.

Psalm 91:

BLOOM WHERE YOU ARE PLANTED

Are you content with your life, or do you often think about moving away to a more beautiful place, or some place that is more fun, more "something" that you don't think you have now?

There was a man who had a lovely family, a good job, and a nice home. He had literally hundreds of friends and people who admired and appreciated him. Still, he was never content. He often talked about taking his family to live on a sailboat, and having the children go to school wherever they docked.

"Or," he mused, "we could move to another country." That sort of talk made his family feel unsettled and insecure.

I live in the High Desert of Southern California. God has called me to live in this place. This I know. I have so many reasons to believe this, beginning with the time my husband, Jim, found a job here.

He came to the desert to apply for a job in a junior high school that he learned had an opening for a math teacher. He was not impressed with the interview or the school as he saw it. On the way out of town, he saw a sign that read "Victor Valley College, 5 miles."

He had nothing to lose, so he turned around and drove there. When he walked into the administration office, he asked, "Do you have any openings in the Math department?"

"We might have," was the answer. "What else do you teach?"

"I am qualified in Math, German and Data Processing."

He noticed the surprised look on the woman's face. She revealed that a man had just left the college to take another position. He had taught Math, German and Data Processing, and they expected to hire three people to replace him.

Jim applied, and got the job immediately. Now we must find a home for our family. He had been unemployed for a few months, due to an illness, which meant that our funds were limited.

We looked at several places, then my husband remembered a remark he had heard as he left the college administration office.

"If you are looking for a house, I have one for sale," said a secretary named Jodi.

He called Jodi and made an appointment for us to see the home that afternoon. We walked through the front door and already felt this place was to be ours. After we looked through it all, and discovered it was even more than we had hoped to find, we asked what the down payment would be.

"I figured with the points and the closing costs, we would need …" and she gave us a figure.

Jim and I looked at each other. It was the exact amount we had put aside for a down payment. We told her we really wanted the place and needed to get our funds together. She said she had another man that had seen the home and was coming back with his wife later in the day.

"Give me a dollar," she suggested, "and I will tell him I have a deposit on it."

A few weeks later, we moved in with great excitement, knowing that was where God planted us. We lived in that home for more than twenty years.

They are like a tree planted by streams of water, which yields its fruit in season...

Psalm 1:3

ADOPTED

The mama finch came back. She had been gone for more than a week and she returned to the two nests —one with 3 little eggs and one with four - which she had been warming for weeks. But the nests were gone. They had simply disappeared. The daddy finch came back the next day and together they searched. He perched on the wind chimes nearby and sang a song of mourning. What could have happened to their babies?

This was the scene on my patio. I am afraid that I was the one who moved the nests. The mama finch had seemingly disappeared, and the eggs were dry.

This episode of the finches returning home to find empty nests, reminded me of my own beginnings.

My twin sister and I were removed from our home when we were one year old. We had been neglected to the point that we did not sit up, or even crawl. Crib babies, we were called.

It seems that the authorities took us when our mother was away. When she came home, she found an empty crib, an empty nest. I can only imagine how devastated – how utterly destroyed - she must have been.

We were soon adopted by a wonderful man and woman, who desperately wanted children, and we were raised in a loving home.

God, our Father in heaven, adopts us as His own when we take His outstretched hand.

When we accept Christ, we become "adopted" children of God, members of His family. The Holy Spirit Himself testifies to our status as God's children.

See Romans 8:15, which shows that as we are adopted into the family of God, we are as a child who needs to grow and develop. Our position is one of full privilege.

BIND US TOGETHER

Christian Singles group at our church was diverse, with varying ages and backgrounds. One year, when it was time to welcome a new set of officers, it was my task, as the outgoing leader, to install the new board.

We lit candles, and charged the new board with certain responsibilities. As the end of the ceremony, we sang "Bind Us Together," during which time I intertwined string around everyone in the room, so that we were all "bound together" at the end of the song.

After we untangled ourselves, a member of the group asked if she could have the string. I had no further use for it and said of course, wondering what in the world she wanted with a ball of string.

A few weeks later, she presented me with the answer. She had used the string to crochet a large, round doily for me. That was 25 years ago and I have it to this day. It graces my round coffee table.

It gives meaning to being bound together with Christ. We were bound as a group of singles, then as friends in the Lord. Each time I see this doily, I think of my friend, who loved me enough to make the doily, and of that group of people who came together in Christian love.

...Whatever you bind on earth will be bound in heaven...

Matthew 16: 19

I look forward to that!

BE CONTENT WHEREVER YOU ARE

When our daughter was moving with her family across country, we had the family over for a farewell picnic in the backyard.

After we ate and visited, it was time to say goodbye. We held hands and gathered in a circle under the old apple tree for a send-off. My husband opened his Bible for a reading. We were, of course, expecting him to say something profound.

He said that, when he was in the Army Air Corps, he discovered the verses where Paul talked about learning to be content in whatever state he was in. "Well," said my husband, "I was in the state of Louisiana and I wanted to be in California, so it wasn't easy to be content!"

Not that I speak in respect of want: for I have learned, in whatsoever state I am, therewith to be content. Philippians 4:11 (KJV)

FIRE!

White flakes are floating through the air, but it is not snowing. The sun isobscured to near oblivion, but it is not cloudy. It is a hot August day, and raging fires are burning all around us. Smoke and falling ashes surround our desert valley.

We are praying for the people who must evacuate where the fires are closing in. Some, who stayed to save their homes, have not only failed to do so, but have been badly burned – or worse.

It is a scary, sad, sense of devastation that comes over us, although we are sure to be safe here, 50 or 60 miles away from the closest fire. Safe, but unsettled.Unscathed, but consumed with the destruction, and the plight of others.

The fires are necessary, they say. Some of the brush is 30 feet tall and has not burned for 60 years. Before the area was civilized, oh, so long ago, the fire could have - and would have - burned on until it burned itself out, clearing out the trees and scrub brush without hurting anyone. Such fires are natural - unless set by a human being.

We wonder why it must be so. Life offers so many questions that cannot be answered by us humans. Unanswered questions can lead us to trust and faith. That is where God comes in. But of course, he is already here.

In times like this, when we feel we have nowhere to turn, we can turn to God. He has the solution for dealing with all of it.

Hear us, O Shepherd of Israel...Awaken your might; come and save us. Restore us, O God; make your face shine upon us, that we may be saved.

Psalm 80: 1 - 4

BROKEN CHAINS

"I saw an apple," she said. "The apple was cut open with the seeds exposed, and one seed looked rotten." She continued, "A hand appeared and removed the bad seed."

Wow! We were a group of seven women, sitting in a circle for prayer. The occasion was the annual conference on prayer and healing, and this was the daily time for everyone to join assigned groups for confidential prayer requests, followed by specific prayers.

The subject of mental illness came up. I could relate to this subject because my husband had been schizophrenic/manic-depressive, and eventually died from an episode. My children were approaching the age where I thought that if this disorder were going to manifest in any of them, it would probably happen soon.

I did not want them to suffer what their father had. He had many episodes of euphoria mixed with fear; of thinking he was Jesus, or of being so depressed that nothing could amuse him.

Therefore, I told my story and asked the group to pray for my family's protection from any further evidence of this illness.

One of them put oil on my forehead, and we all bowed in prayer. Afterward, a woman told of her vision of half an apple. Among the apple seeds was one that was bad. She saw a hand reaching in to lift out the bad seed. Another said that she saw chains being broken; and still another related that she, too, had seen the broken chains. Wow.

Wow, indeed. I came home and told my children that they would be all right. And they have been. Praise God.

"Is any one of you sick? He should call the elders to pray over him and anoint him with oil in the name of the Lord. And the prayer offered in faith will make the sick person well; the Lord will raise him up."

James 5: 14

SPAGHETTI SAUCE AND JOY

The air filled with wonderful aromas. I was sautéing garlic and onions in the process of making spaghetti sauce. I loved the smells of cooking, but my husband did not. When he sauntered into the kitchen he asked, "What is that awful smell?"

I assured him that he would like the end product, and suggested that he just go out on the patio for a while.

"And please close the screen door on your way out, because flies are coming in."

"They'll be dead in a minute!" he grumbled.

I got such a kick out of this. He always had a cute sense of humor, but this time I was sure he was more serious than kidding.

This is a reminder that things do not always end up the way we expect. The spaghetti sauce has ingredients that might not be so tasty on their own, but in combination with other things, it can become a rich and delectable treat.

Isn't life like that? Our troubles, our problems, the many ingredients of our lives may not be pleasant as they happen. However, we can learn from them, and in the end, if we mix all the experiences together and stir them around, our lives can become so much richer.

It is important to recognize that we are the sum total of all things that happen to us. The way we react to events has a direct effect, not only on our lives, but on that of others, as well. This is not a profound statement, but something to consider seriously.

…Consider it pure joy…when you face trials of many kinds…

James 1:3

SOLID GOLD

The man had a vision. Or was it a dream?

He was standing on desolate desert land. Nearby was a large mound of red dirt - crusty, muddied by rain, then dried, and muddied again.

In the distance, radiating in waves of heat, was – what? A flag? A sheet? It floated in slow motion towards the man, ever more near, until it took the shape of a human. It was Jesus, shrouded in flowing white.

As He closed in on the crust-covered form, He danced slowly around the mound. Pieces of crust broke away, and fell to the ground.

As they separated, there was a familiarity. What was it? Who was it? The gleam of gold was blinding.

Then he saw. It was a form of *the man, himself*, and it was solid gold.

God knew that this man, my pastor friend Gifford, was upright. That he loved God and worshiped him. Gifford was humbled that, in spite of his transgressions, God saw him as pure gold.

But he knows the way that I take; when he has tested me, I will come forth as solid gold.

Job 23:10

DAD

My father-in-law was in his 80's when he came to stay with me for a week while my mother-in-law was traveling. Since I lived alone, I looked forward to the company of this dear man.

I hadnot realized that he was becoming a bit "old." His mind was not as sharp as I remembered, but he functioned well enough.

As I left for work each morning, I would leave him various instructions: "Don't turn this on. "(He did). "Wait until I get home to do that." (He did not).

After a few days of frustration, I had a revelation. This good man is like Jesus, I thought. That's who he is. This man is like Jesus, and he is here for me to care for. Oh, what a difference that made.

From then on, we had a wonderful time. We watched old Jack Benny shows and he laughed so hard he fell off his chair. I began to love him more than I ever had.

He really missed his wife, Bunny, and wrote little notes to her every day. On Saturday morning, I awoke and entered the living room. There was Dad, dressed in a three-piece suit and tie, suitcase beside him.

"My goodness," I exclaimed, "You are all dressed up!"

"I'm ready to go home," he said. "Bunny is coming home today."

"Oh, Dad, I'm so sorry but that is not until tomorrow."

I encouraged him to change clothes, then come and help me rake leaves in the front yard. We worked together, and I saw that he was getting warm and tired. I went inside and made a pitcher of lemonade. I took him a tall tumbler of the ice cold drink and suggested he sit in the rocker on the front stoop. He did so gratefully, pulled out his handkerchief and wiped his brow.

"Whew!" he said. "Now I know how the slaves felt!"

Oh, my goodness. Bless his heart. I realized that we had raked enough leaves for one day. This still makes me smile.

The next morning, I awoke and entered the living room. There was Dad, again dressed in three-piece suit and tie, suitcase beside him. This time I said, "Yes, today is the day. I will take you home."

He slept the entire 150 miles home. I do not believe he had slept much all week, anticipating the end of the separation from his sweet Bunny.

I tell you the truth, whatever you did for one of the least of these… you did for me. Matthew 25:40 NIV

It is important to try to see others as Jesus sees them. After all, God made us all – even you, even me.

Through Him all things were made…

John 1:3

SANDRA

Sandra was one of those people who comeinto our lives that are just not our favorite. I call them my "irregular people. " It isn't that Sandra was not a nice person. She was very nice and sweet, pleasant, even, and very smart. There was just something about her.

She often stopped by the house without warning, and she usually had a gift - maybe a lug of peaches or a bouquet of flowers. We knew she intended to stay a while, as she held her purse in her hand.

We sometimes had to tell her, "Sandra, this is not a good time," and off she would go with a smile.

When we had gatherings that included her, she leaned in on private family conversations. She seemed to want to be a part of everything in our lives, and it was sometimes just too much for us.

We watched her gain weight as she continued to eat all the wrong things.

"No common sense," we said.

We were frustrated as she made unwise financial decisions that drained her lifesavings, in spite of our sage advice.

"She will be sorry," we clucked.

She had a way of making us all feel loved by her - and special. - greeting us enthusiastically, as if we were just the person she was hoping to see. That could be embarrassing, since she was still, somehow, "irregular."

Her head began to hurt. She was confused. She lost her way to familiar places. Something was very wrong. We rushed her to the emergency room, and learned that she had a brain tumor. The next thing we knew, she was in surgery. After anxious days of waiting, we realized that she would never wake up. She was on her way to meet her Lord, who lifted her into His arms with no bias.

At her memorial service, we learned who Sandra really was, before the tumor, before we met her. She had been a vivacious and intelligent woman, successful in business. She was a loving daughter who, when her parents both died, was left alone, save her friends, whom she adopted as family.

Family. That was us. If only we had known.

She wanted to belong, and when she sometimes interrupted the flow of our lives, we could barely tolerate it. Looking back, how would we have responded had we known of the tumor? Would we have endured her intrusions?

For heaven's sake, what was bad about being friendly, cheerful, generous, and all the good things we saw in Sandra? Was she really so disruptive? God, forgive us.

Maybe we will get a second chance somewhere along the way. When we interrupt God, He does not say, "This is not a good time, Mychild, come back later." We can come to the Lord anytime. We can lay all of our burdens at His feet. We can give Him our very lives. He accepts us as we are, because He knows us inside and out, and loves us anyway.

Praise God.

"I will call them 'my people' who are not my people; and I will call her 'my loved one' who is not my loved one."

Hosea 2:23

Praise God, indeed!

GET IN THE BOAT

"Is this the job for me, Lord, or did I misread you?"

The job had almost come to me, rather than my seeking it. I wandered into an office and saw a friend.

"Are you looking for a job?" she asked.

"I could be," I responded. "I really just came into ask for directions."

"We have openings, if you are interested. Let me introduce you to our manager."

That was how it began. The manager and I hit it off. I took some tests, and the next thing I knew, I was on a plane to Kansas City for three weeks of school.

I liked the job, but a few weeks into it, I began to doubt whether I could make a success of it. I was struggling.

About that time, a class called "Stretching" was offered for women at the church. I signed up.

One evening, instructions were to scatter around the room so we would have some privacy. The leader gave us a certain scripture to read and interpret for how it fit into our daily lives.

My assignment was in Matthew:

Then he got into the boat and his disciples followed him. Suddenly a furious storm came up on the lake, so that the waves swept over the boat. But Jesus was sleeping. The disciples went and woke him, saying, "Lord, save us! We're going to drown!"

He replied, "You of little faith, why are you so afraid?" Then he got up and rebuked the winds and the waves, and it was completely calm

Matthew 8:23 - 26

I read it, and understood. God just told me to get into the boat and trust him. He did not promise smooth sailing. Even the disciples had difficulty in putting their complete faith in him, despite the miracles they witnessed.

I stayed with the job, and eventually won awards for my work.

Thank you, Father.

GOD KNEW

It was one of those bad days - at least, in my mind it was. I was crying, and feeling hopeless when the phone rang. My friends, Burt and Margie, were on the line together, and they called to see how things were going with me, alone in a new city.

It felt so good to talk with friends just when I needed them, and I told them what had upset me. Before the conversation was over, Margie quoted scripture to me, and I was comforted.

Margie passed away a few years later. Surprisingly, about five years after her death, I found myself married to Burt and living in their home. Burt and I knew without a doubt that God had put us in each other's lives.

We were not alike, and had never been interested in each other in such a manner in the 30 years we had been acquainted. This new love was God given.

As we settled into a rhythm as husband and wife, the scripture I had heard from Margie came back to me:

"For I know the plans I have for you," declares the Lord, "plans to prosper you and not to harm you, plans to give you hope and a future." Jeremiah 29:11

Here I was, living in Margie's house with Margie's husband. She couldnot have known how prophetic her scripture reference for me would be. None of us could have. Ah, but God knew.

NOT YET

My husband's health was failing. His Parkinson's disease had taken its toll, and it appeared that Burt would not last much longer. The hospice nurse, Bob, took me to the kitchen, opened the refrigerator, and took out The Box. It contained such things as morphine to make a patient comfortable in the final days or hours. He instructed me on the use of it all, and of course, told me to call if I needed help.

This was a scary time. Burt and I had talked about death – his death. How it would be for Burt to go to heaven and be with Jesus, his father, his first wife, and all who had gone before him.

One night, when I sat on the edge of his bed, I asked him, "How much time do you think you have left?"

"Not much," he said.

"Well, as I see it, you have a choice. You can go home to Jesus now, or you can wait until your daughter comes in two weeks, so you can see her again."

After a few minutes, I asked him, "So what's it gonna be?"

He gave me a strong "thumbs up". I kissed him goodnight, and went upstairs to bed.

During the night, I did my usual checking on him numerous times, and each time, he was sleeping soundly, for a change. Often he would be wide awake, staring at the ceiling.

I awoke to a sunny morning. I got up and brushed my teeth, then headed downstairs to see how Burt was doing. I was astonished to see him sitting up in bed! He nearly shouted, "Good morning!"

Wow! Hallelujah! I did not know what had happened, but I was sure a happy wife. I fixed him breakfast, and brought him the paper, which he read for the first time in several days. Whew! This was good.

A few days later, I squeezed in beside him on the little hospital bed. I liked doing this partly because he could hear me talking in his ear, and partly because I just loved being close to him.

"We thought we were going to lose you last week," I said.

"So did I."

"Really? What thoughts did you have during that time?"

"I dreamed about my dad a lot." His dad had Parkinson's, and died about 35 years before this.

"What sort of dreams?"

"I dreamed he came to get me, and I wouldn't go."

Burt lived an additional eight months.

You, O Lord, keep my lamp burning; my God turns my darkness into light.

Psalm 18:28

GRACE AND MERCY

My twin sister called me to say that an angiogram that morning showed that she must have heart surgery right away. I e-mailed friends to ask for prayers.

Many of them responded that they would pray for her. I printed all of those e-mails and made a collage of them to mail to her.

After the surgery, the doctor said that he had found a blood clot in an artery that meant she was only minutes from death.

She told me later that she was so grateful for "all those lovely people" praying for her. She said she had sensed angels in her midst ever since the prayers began, and is sure that is why she is alive today.

We had just become sisters, really, for the first time in our adult lives. We were never close, (although we are twins), even in childhood, and for 20 years we didn't even see each other.

However, one year, I flew to Texas to be with her for our birthday, and we have become closer.

It is wonderful to have a sister! I want to keep her, now that we know each other as women.

"...In your great mercy, you did not put an end to them or abandon them, for you are a gracious and merciful God."

Nehemiah 9:31

SISTER-FRIENDS

M any good friends have blessed my life. The following three women left too soon.

Mary

"One.two, three…" I count slowly, as I hold down the "on" button of the coffee grinder. "…10, 11, 12, 13. There, Mary, that's for you."

This is a morning ritual as I grind the beans and remember my dear sister - friend, Mary. She gave me my first coffee grinder on a visit to my home one day. I asked her how long I should grind the beans and she answered thoughtfully, "Thirteen, um, yes, count to thirteen."

Mary was one of those sweet women who would not hurt a fly. I can still recall the sound of her laugh. She laughed at herself a lot, at her mistakes and what she thought might seem odd to others. When I introduced her to other friends, they warmed to her immediately. She was comfortable and easy to be around. Mary was a loyal friend, and much like a sister to me.

We met when she moved to town with her two lovely daughters and her husband, who came to be the assistant pastor at our church in Arizona. My husband and I liked them right away, and the four of us became good friends.

Soon, Mary and I decided we would like to meet every week for prayer and conversation. She was an unassuming, loving, and caring woman. We were, indeed, sisters in Christ.

Later, my family and I moved to Southern California. Soon, Mary and her family also moved to the area, and lived about an hour's drive away. She and I picked up where we had left off, just not as often. We would meet for lunch somewhere in between our two towns, and visit until tables were being prepared for dinner. We joked that the restaurant should charge us rent.

We both moved again, she to Northern California, and I, single now, moved to Nevada. She came there to stay with me, and brought me the coffee grinder. We painted my new townhouse kitchen together, laughing and chatting our way through the white enamel mess, then admiring our work a few days later. I hugged her goodbye after a week, and knew that God had blessed me.

Later that year, she and her husband were on a trip that led them close to where I lived. Mary called to tell me that she so wanted to come by, but her husband felt they should go on home.

That Thanksgiving, after a sumptuous dinner with her husband, children and young grandson, she sat on the stairs in the mountain cabin that was now home.

"I'm so glad we're all here together," she said in her sweet voice, and then she was gone. Mary just lay down and died.

I could hardly believe my ears when I got the call. I had hugged her goodbye, not imagining that it would be for the last time. Twenty years later, my heart breaks still.

Rowena

"Annie!" she said, with suspicion in her voice. "Where are my rings?"

Rowena always took her wedding rings off when she played the piano, because they slipped around and got in her way. Tonight she was accompanying our singing group for rehearsal. I often would swipe the rings while she was not looking. It was a game we played. Actually, it was a game *I* played, leaving her no choice. However, the first time I took the rings, she panicked.

We had met many years previously. She was the church secretary and eventually the organist. Since I was active in many church events, I saw her often, and we became good friends. Our birthdays were one day apart in November, although in different years, and we were both born in Oklahoma. We invented the nickname Sister Scorpiokies – Scorpios and Okies.

Rowena had a phenomenal memory. She somehow managed to lock into her brain the phone numbers of all 1000, or so, church members. If you asked her for the number of someone new, she might not know it. She said that was because she had not yet focused on it…but you knew she soon would.

We both enjoyed hosting dinner parties. One difference, however, was that Rowena insisted on having an even number around the table. She might call for a recipe of mine, and add, "Sorry, Annie, you're not invited to this one." I understood. When my husband was alive, we were both invited.

One memorable evening, she invited several mutual friends to her home for dinner and a movie. After dinner, we all sprawled on the living room floor and waited for the movie to begin. She had kept the title a secret and we were to see who would be the first to recognize it.

On the screen appeared a beautiful sunrise, accompanied by a soft overture. In a few minutes, someone called out, "Fiddler on the Roof!" Having seen it more than once, and all of us being musicians, we sang and spoke the lines along with the actors. It was good fun.

Rowena was a good organist, a phenomenal secretary, and a wonderful friend. We leaned on each other through many difficult situations. That's what sisters do.

She had chronic headaches for years, and when they got too painful, she finally went for an exam. The doctor said that she should have brain surgery. When the long procedure was over, the doctors had removed a vital part of her brain, and this brilliant woman was left in a vegetative state. Thus endedher meaningful life. Her devoted husband cared for her during the next few years, until she passed away.

I cried as I sang with the choir at her funeral. It was so hard to say goodbye.

Lisa Lotte

Lisa Lotte came to live with the Miner family before I married into it. She was an exchange student from a small town named Aars, in Northern Denmark. A darling personality and a sense of humor endeared her to us all. Her giving heart and a pretty face made her a popular senior at the American high school. We called her Lottie.

I was engaged to Jim Miner when she arrived in America, and it was my privilege to get to know her. We struck a friendship rather quickly, as I was only two years older than she.

Our wedding day came, and Lottie had a surprise for us. She had contacted her mother to have a unique gift made. It was a flat, treated hide of a goat. Written at the top, was *GoesteSkind, Til Ann og Jim frajeresDanskesoester, Lotte.* "Guest Skin, to Ann and Jim from there Danish sister, Lotte."

After those words was a Danish flag in traditional red and white, followed by the wedding date. She explained that it was customary for the Danes to have a guest skin hung in their homes. All of our wedding guests signed it, in place of a guest book.

Jim and I hung that skin on the wall by the front door for 18 years, encouraging our visitors to sign in or out, until it was beginning to fall apart. Folded and put away now, it is, these 50 years later, too precious to discard.

In those early days, Lotte stayed with me now and then while Jim was gone to basic training for the army. About six months into her one-year exchange, Lottie's mother passed away suddenly. She had to make a decision whether to stay in San Diego, or go back to Denmark for the funeral. The consequences of her leaving California early would be that she could not come back. It was not an easy decision for an 18-year old, but she opted to let her mother be buried without her. In retrospect, it was a wise decision.

One of the favorite things of us Miners was for Lotte to make Ebelskivers, a round ball-shaped sort of Danish pancake. She would make a few at a time, and place them on a towel on the counter to cool. We would all casually walk by and take one. By the time the next batch was ready, the first batch was gone. When she was completely finished cooking, she was lucky to have one left for herself. We knew she was pleased that we loved them, and she was always a good sport.

Soon after her year was up and she was back home, I had the privilege to visit her little village in Denmark. I learned that she was a leader in her community and a very mature young woman. She was loved and popular in her home setting, not unlike San Diego's response to her.

She had learned to speak English well, and her former English teacher in Denmark teased that she now spoke American English. He had taught English with British phonetics.

Over the years, I was able to return to Denmark with all the family, including my grown children. Those visits are among our most cherished memories.

Lottie's death was sudden, similar to Mary's. One minute she seemed fine, the next, she was gone. It took her son two weeks to get the energy to call and tell me. Although she was married to a strong and wonderful man, Henrik, she was the center of the family. Her three children and Henrik all depended on her wisdom and leadership.

I remember our last embrace. I didn't want it to end, as I did not know when I would ever see her again. As it happened, I never did.

I will miss all my sister friends forever, with a grateful heart for the blessings of having loved them. I know that we will meet again in heaven, not having lost a beat in our relationships.

A friend loves at all times...

Proverbs 17:17

SUZANNE

It was dark. Dark in my heart. Dark in my soul. I could hardly breathe.

I felt exposed, naked. It seemed that everyone knew.

Some believed what they read on the front page of the newspaper.

Some wondered whether it was even possible.

Others realized it could never be true.

My child was in trouble, and I was helpless to help. My heart felt as if it were broken in half.

Friends were there for support and prayer, but how would we get through this? I did not want to go out into the community. In the grocery store, I focused on the shelves to avoid speaking to anyone. I continued to go to church. Most worshipers looked away. I looked straight ahead or kept my head bowed in prayer.

Then one Sunday morning after the church service, Suzanne came to me with a look of compassion. She hugged me and held me close. No words were needed. Just her affirmation of love and understanding were enough. Her kindness and gentleness warmed and comforted me.

In my great pain, I turned to God. I looked to the Psalms for strength and understanding. I came to know them well during that tumultuous time.

"Have mercy on me, O God, have mercy on me, for in you my soul takes refuge. I will take refuge in the shadow of your Wings until the disaster has passed. Psalm 57:1

The disaster passed. I must remember to tell Suzanne how much her loving kindness meant to me.

ASK

Please, Lord, let them find it.

We were preparing the old house for sale. The numerous rules and regulations for selling it were overwhelming. We repaired, painted, or replaced several things. I found plenty of opportunities to ask God for help.

One thing of immediate concern on this day was the septic tank. Upon inspection by the officials, it reportedly needed to be replaced. Doing so promised to be a daunting and expensive endeavor. We would have to cut down a tree, remove a section of the vine-covered fence, and destroy the grass and sprinkler system in that area of the yard.

My husband, Burt, was certain that he remembered putting in a new tank several years earlier, but he could not remember where it was and the man from "Honest John" could not locate it.

While we pondered what to do the next few days, Burt's grown children came for the weekend. They, too, were certain that a new tank had been installed. But where?

The following Monday morning I called Honest John and asked if he could come out and try again.

While Burt and Honest John continued the search, I cleaned off the top shelf of a closet. Feeling somewhat stressed, I prayed.

Please Lord, let them find it.

I pulled on one loose ribbon, and everything came tumbling down off the shelf. In the pile on the floor was an envelope. I opened it, and found a dozen or more photos taken when the newer septic tank was installed! The pictures showed the exact location.

I could not wait to tell Burt. Clutching the envelope, I ran out the back door.

"I think you'll find these useful," I grinned, and handed him the pictures. We were ecstatic.

We would have found the photos eventually, but it was urgent that we find them that day, before we began preparations to install a new tank.

He answered their prayer because they trusted in him.
1 Chronicles 5:20

REMINISCING

When I fixed breakfast for my visiting grown daughter that morning, memories from another life, long ago, came gently floating into the kitchen.

I was cooking for three young children and my husband. They gathered around the kitchen table wiggling and giggling in anticipation, as the wonderful fragrance of bacon and pancakes filled the room.

Bacon, crisp and lots of it, was always a treat. If I wanted my share, I had to put a couple of slices aside for myself. Pancakes in those days still required my making a mess of the first two or three, until I got the grill temperature just right.

I wonder if I appreciated the experience in those days as much as I would appreciate it today. How I miss it. The laughter, the teasing, the requests for "more?" "Yes, please." My eyes moisten as I remember, realizing how time skitters away while we aren't watching.

I long for such a time again. I want "do-overs." I want to make it better for everyone. To raise my children with more wisdom and to love them more softly, with a gentler voice.

Maybe that's why God made grandparents.

There is a time for everything, and a season for every activity under heaven...Ecclesiastes 3:1

INTERCESSORY PRAYER

"Oh, no! It's too late!" I wailed. "I waited too long and now it's too late!"

I had coughed up blood, and was certain that I had cancer from smoking. It frightened me, of course, and I threw the remainder of the pack of cigarettes in the trash.

Later that day, I realized that the blood had not come from my lungs, and it was a false alarm. I decided that I would quit smoking, anyway. I had quit many times over the years, so I knew I could do it.

That conviction lasted just long enough for me to get to work the next day and bum a cigarette from a colleague.

"*Blaack!*" I exclaimed. "It tastes like weeds!"

That was that. Not only did I quit smoking, but it was easy this time. I had no desire for another cigarette, nor have I ever since then.

About three months after this incident, I bumped into a friend at church.

"Have you lost weight?" she asked.

"Why, yes, I have," I replied. "I lost weight <u>and</u> I quit smoking. What do you think of that?"

"You quit smoking? We prayed for that."

I knew that she was a long-time member of a weekly Bible study and prayer group.

"Why, you meddling women, I joked. "Every time I try to start again, I get sick!".

"We prayed that the cigarettes would become as a bitter herb in your mouth."

Wow! I was humbled and in awe. What power their intercessory prayer had. The Lord heard, and a miracle happened.

I thank God that he heard their prayers. I thank Him that He hears us all when we pray. What a privilege to fellowship with the Lord.

I urge, then, first of all, that petitions, prayers, intercession and thanksgiving be made for all people…for kings and all those in authority, that we may live peaceful and quiet lives in all godliness and holiness. This is good, and pleases God our Savior…

1 Timothy 2:1-3

"I PROMISE"

"If you wish to give your life to Christ, raise your hands."

I had already done that, so I kept still. "If you wish to _____, raise your hands."

I raised mine.

As I drove home from church that Sunday evening, I remembered that I had raised my hand, but I had absolutely no recollection of why. What had I promised to God?

Days went by, and I began to notice that something was different. I began to share my faith randomly, which I did not often do. Then one smoldering May morning, I rescued a man who was lost and confused, who had literally been wandering in the desert for five days.

When I found him, he was standing on a bridge, looking up at the sun while he turned in circles. I kept driving, and prayed that someone would help the poor soul. In mere moments, I knew that God had assigned him to me!

I drove the two miles to my home and hurriedly changed into jeans and tennis shoes. I wanted to be able to keep my balance if I needed to defend myself… After I made ice water and a cheese sandwich, I quickly soaked a towel in cold water, snatched some fruit from the kitchen counter, and rushed back to my car. My heart pounded as I headed back toward the bridge to search for him, afraid that I had missed a chance to help …the God-given chance. I found him about three blocks down the street from the bridge, standing on the sidewalk.

His clothes were thick with desert sand and dirt. His sandaled feet were blackened with asphalt dust. I learned later that he had walked there from about 60 miles away. How he got up and over the long Cajon Pass that led from his town to ours is still a mystery to me.

Where had he slept for those five days? Had he even eaten?

His thinning, blond, straight hair was shoulder length in the back, and deeply receding in the front. He had missing teeth, and, generally looked undernourished and unhealthy.

I approached him and offered him the towel. He took the cold, wet cloth and rubbed it all over his face – then burst into jubilant laughter! It felt so good.

"Are you a cop?" he asked.

"No," I replied.

"Who are you?"

"Just a friend."

He looked around him, and then asked, "Do you know where Mary's Hospital is?"

"Yes, do you need to go there?"

"I need to get some medicine. I went to the other hospital and they said to go to Mary's."

When I asked what kind of medicine he needed, he listed some that I recognized to be for mental illness. Now what? If I gave him directions and just drove away, he would have to walk a mile over a steep hill in the sweltering heat. If I let him get into my car and drove him there, would I be safe?

I knew what I must do. I invited him into the car. I uttered quietly, "Jesus stay with me. Jesus, please stay with me."

Aware that my wallet was on the center console, I moved it to my left side. He noticed. "Do you have any money?"

No."

"Are you married?"

"Uh-huh." I was not married, but I felt safer saying that I was.

We reached the small hospital, and I tried to get him into the emergency room so he could be examined and given the meds that he requested.

The doctors would not see him. They said that there was a possibility of him having other drugs in his system and they did not want to prescribe any medications that would interact negatively.

This was another challenge. I had expected the hospital to take the responsibility from me. I needed to get home and prepare for my daughter's going-away party that evening. Now I was stuck.

I asked him questions about where he lived. I discovered that he and his wife lived in a small residential home for mentally ill people. Somehow, I was able to get a phone number for that home. I talked with a nurse, then with his wife. She asked me if I could keep him for a few days until she could work out a way to come for him.

I explained that I was just a citizen who had picked him up to go to the hospital, that the hospital would not take him, and that I had no way of accommodating him myself. It seemed to be one dilemma after another.

We finally came to a decision that seemed feasible. I called the sheriff's office and asked them to come and pick him up, keep him overnight, and put him on a bus for home the next morning.

I explained to Ron – I had asked his name – that he would be taken to the jail, but that he was not in trouble. It was just a place to stay overnight. And he would see his wife the next day. He seemed to understand.

While we waited for his ride, we had limited conversation.

"Your husband died, didn't he?"

"What makes you say that?"

"Just something I am thinking."

I wrote a letter to the deputy who would be coming for him. I explained the situation, emphasizing that Ron was not a dangerous man, but a man in danger. I noted where I had found him, where he was from, and everything I had learned about him. I ended the note with, "Please be gentle with him."

By the time the deputy came, Ron was weakened and confused. I felt so bad for him.

I followed the patrol car to the red light, and saw that the deputy was reading the note. That was a relief.

Later in the week, I phoned to see that Ron had made it safely home.

Two weeks later, I phoned him on his birthday. He vaguely remembered the incident, but I didn't care. I knew that I was just following orders.

This rescue cost me the rest of the day, and it was so unlike me that I went to my pastor to ask what on earth I had promised that Sunday evening. This was the scripture:

And {God} looked for one who would make up the hedge and stand in the gap...Ezekiel 22:30

There it was. I was to stand in the gap and help others get across. Now I see so many ways to do that. I can pray for them; hold their hands as they cross the chasm of sorrow, or fear or pain; listen; lay on hands for healing; and be open to other needs that God shows me.

I forgot what I had promised that evening, but God remembered. I am so glad that He did.

WHAT COULD GO WRONG IN SPRING?

It's Spring! What could go wrong in Spring?

Maybe that is what the crowds in the streets were thinking when they danced and waved palm branches, as Jesus rode into town on a donkey on that day we now call Palm Sunday. Life was good and gettin' better.

However, all of that changed in the blink of an eye. At least, it seemed that way for a while. Jesus was dead! How could this be? They had just met Him, just come to know who He really was. They had celebrated Him. Life had been good, and was gettin' better.

However, God was in control. He knew what was happening to His Son, and He knew that Easter was coming next. Hewasincontrol.

Things seemed good with us one Palm Sunday when we were with family in Santa Barbara. A grandson, who was a graduating music major at Westmont College, presented his compositions and performances in a concert that was all about his accomplishments.

He performed nearly two hours of choral music, compositions for the carillon, a recorder trio, the piano, an operetta, and so on. We felt good, happy, and blessed. We celebrated with great food on the sidewalks of Santa Barbara. Life was good and gettin' better.

However, all of that changed in the blink of an eye. At least, it seemed that way for a while. When we got home and discovered that we had been robbed, and that my computer with all my writing had been stolen, I wondered, "How could this be?" Hadn't God put it on my heart to write?

I was devastated. Confused.Frustrated.Angry.Sad. I just wanted to go into the closet in a fetal position and suck my thumb, so to speak. Then I remembered: *God is in control.* If He gave me all of those thoughts to write, He would not allow any of the important ones to be taken away. Somehow, they would be restored. In my head or from friends' computers - or not. It was in His hands.

Forgive the analogy. I do not want to seem blasphemous. There is no comparison between the two events, except to remember that GOD IS IN CONTROL! If we allow Him in, allow Him to be a part of our inmost beings, our hourly musings, our daily lives, our loves, our listenings, we will always realize that God is in control.

The Lord has established his throne in heaven, and His kingdom rules over all. Psalm 103:19

MERCIES

"We just ran over your little boy!"

For a dizzying moment, my mind could not grasp what my eyes saw. At my front door stood a man and woman, he holding our chubby little toddler in his arms.

"He was standing beside our driveway and waved to us as we started to back the car out," said the man. "We thought he was out of the way! Then we felt the car run over him! We are so sorry!"

This was my first time to meet Bob and Barbara. We had just moved in to our new home a few days earlier. Their station wage was packed to the hilt in preparation for Boy Scout Camp, where Bob would be Scout Master. This heavy-laden car had just run over our little Jay, whom I should never have let out of my sight.

Jay was not crying, but had a pained look on his face as he reached out for his mama. Somehow, they had run over only the fat of his thigh, and missed the rest of his little body!

We took him immediately to the hospital emergency room. As we waited for answers about his condition, we prayed fervently with our other two pre-school children for our little Jay to be okay.

Jay was okay, thank God. He was only bruised. Years later, he was okay when a drunken driver hit his truck and totaled it, and landed him in the ER once again. In addition, he was okay when he and his brother were seriously injured in a major car accident, rendering him unconscious, with a broken body and badly massacred face.

Yes, he was "okay," for it was after this last incident that he recognized that God must have a plan for him. God had been merciful, and he wanted to "do something for God."

In Lamentations 3:23, Jeremiah tells us *"God's mercies are new every morning."*

They needed to be for my carefree, accident-prone son. Jay kept his promise. He serves the Lord with his own life, and with his music.

Praise you, Father. Amen

WINTER IS COMING!

On the first day of October, I pulled on my warm, fluffy robe, slid into my cozy slippers and schlepped out to the living room. I was about to turn on the fireplace to take the Fall chill out of the air when I noticed the temperature on the indoor thermometer. It was 70 degrees! Well, it *had* been a hot summer.

October in the high desert is the most beautiful, rewarding month of the year for me. Cool nights, warm days, and clear skies. Perfect for working outside. Time to harvest for Fall. Time to plant for Spring. Soon the roses must be pruned.

Nevertheless, for now, for today, I will sit in the sunshine on the swing by the tinkling brook, and watch the bunnies nibble on the melon rinds I left on "their" rock.

I will close my eyes and listen while birds fuss over breakfast and crack open the sunflower seeds in the feeders.

I will praise God for the wonder of it all. It is the Fall of my life, too. Much is behind me, but more is ahead.

I am warmed by thoughts of all that My Father has bestowed upon me. I am excited for what He has placed before me.

Winter is coming, and I am ready for it.

There is a future for the man of peace. Psalm 37:37

www.ingramcontent.com/pod-product-compliance
Lightning Source LLC
Chambersburg PA
CBHW032211040426
42449CB00005B/535